Due Mesi a Roma

A Drawing Collection by Jane Kriss

Book design, layout, and illustrations by Jane Kriss
Photo by Mark Kriss
Special thanks to my son Jesse for his invaluable help in getting this project off the ground.

Second Edition

First edition of 40 books published by Jane Kriss Studio, March 2010

ISBN-10: 0-615-43819-9
ISBN-13: 9780615438191

Cover: View from the Borghese Gardens

For two months in the spring of 2009, my husband Mark and I lived in the Trastevere neighborhood of Rome.

Each day I did a drawing.
My goal was to use daily drawing as a way to stop and focus, in a city so dense with history, texture, and energy. It also kept me connected with friends and family, as a daily on-line post.

I had no idea how much this experience would change my life.

This book is for Mark. And for Rome.

– *Jane Kriss*
March 2010

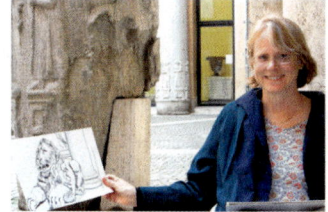

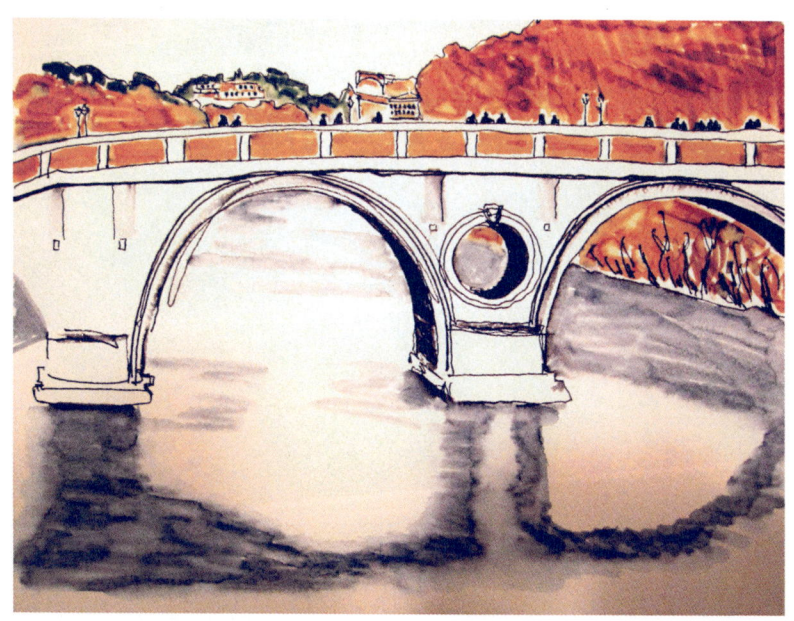

Ponte Sisto, Early March

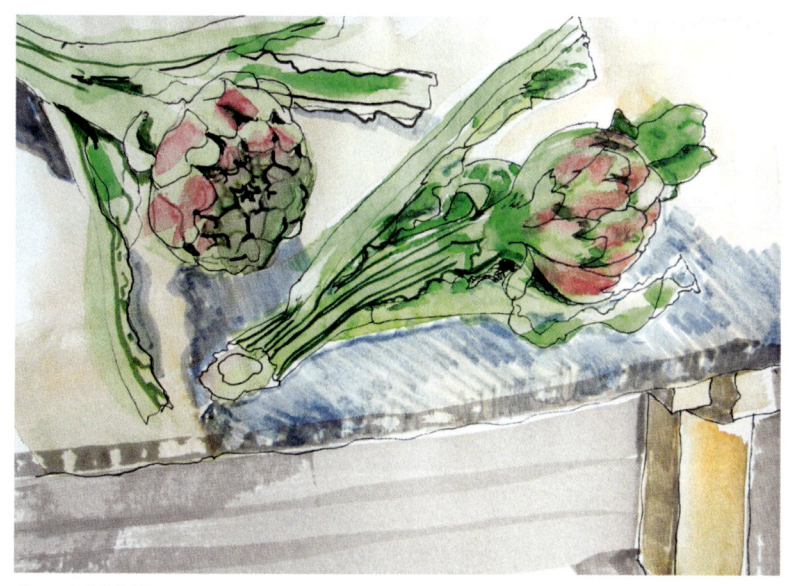

Specialità Romana

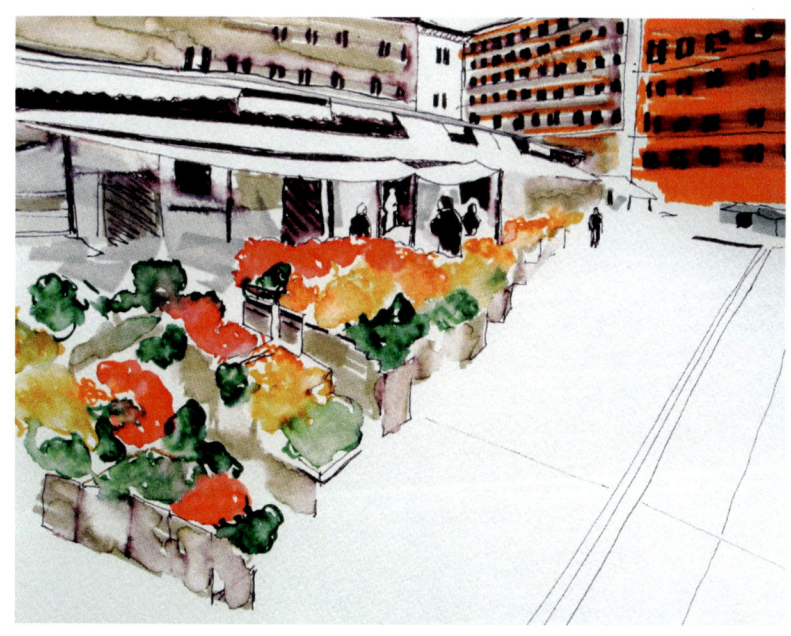

Produce Galore

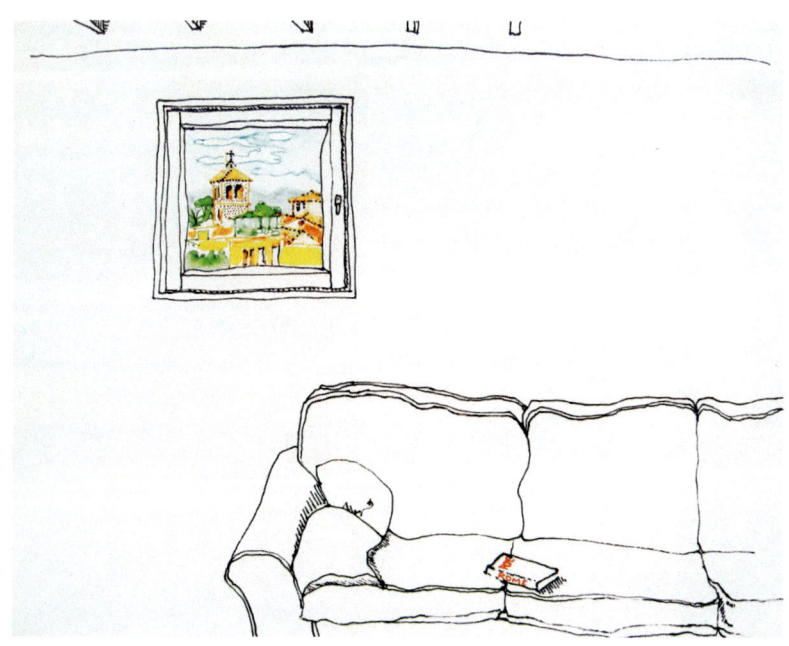

Zen View

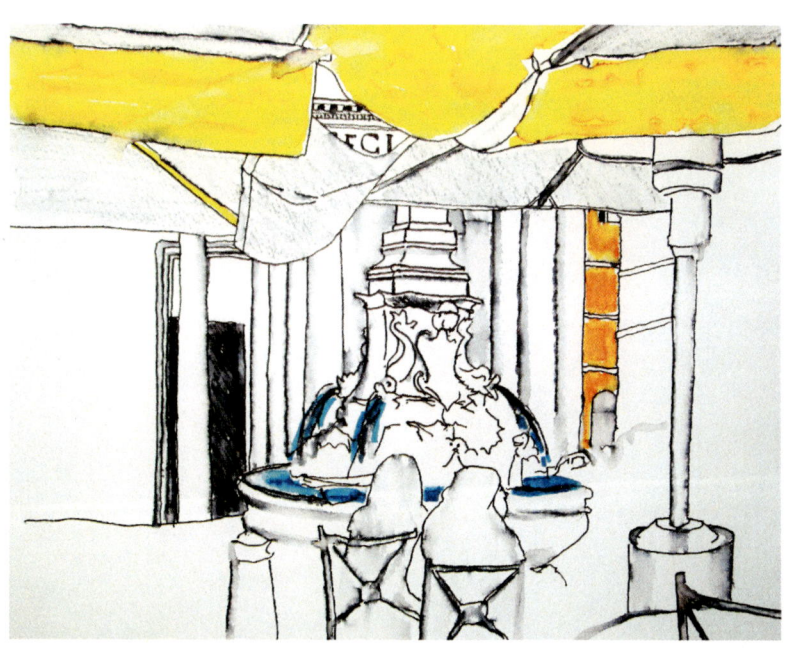

Under Cover at the Pantheon

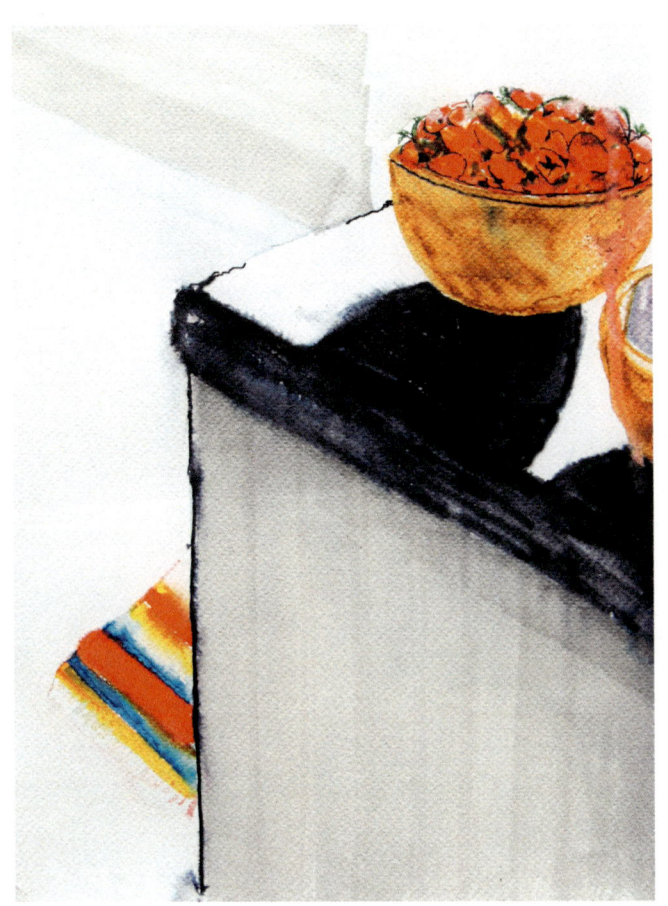

Bright Morning

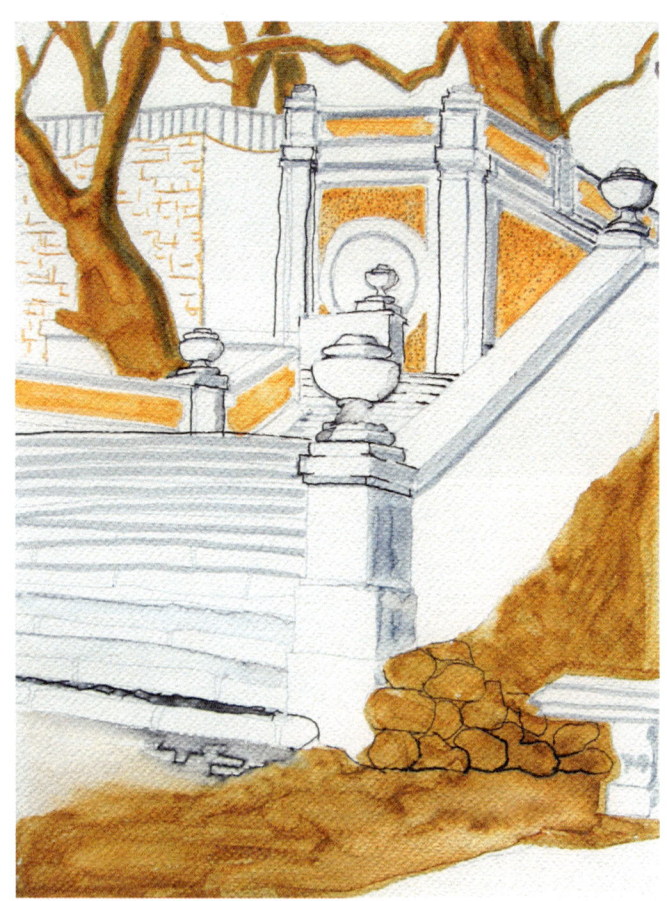

Queen Christina's Staircase

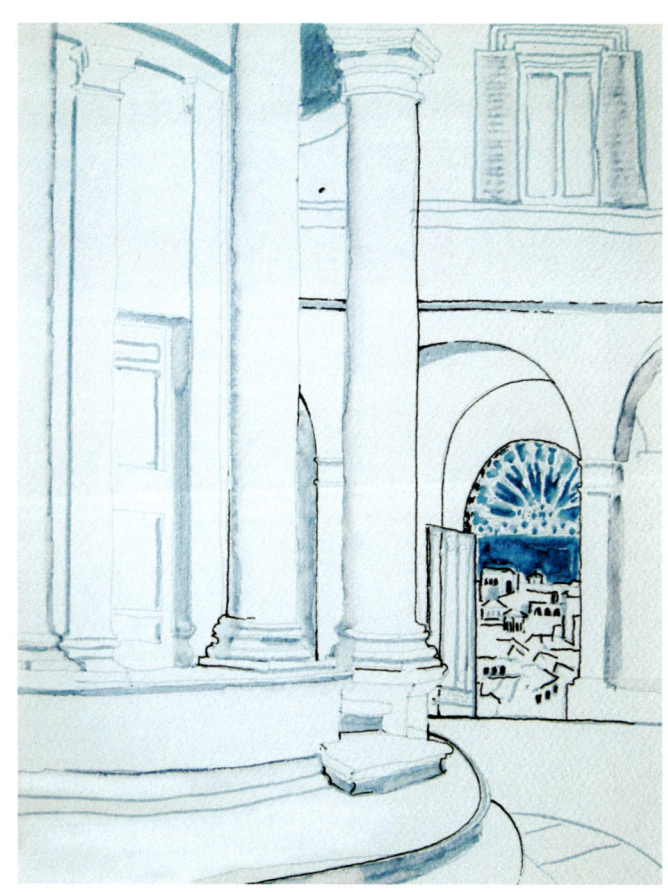

Blue Sky from the Tempietto

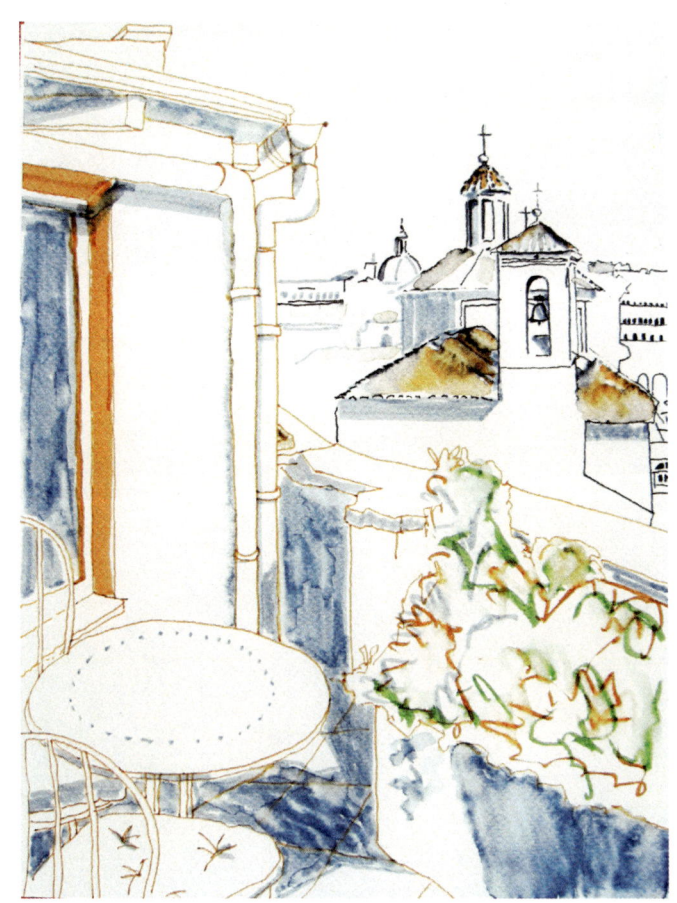

Living Room View #3

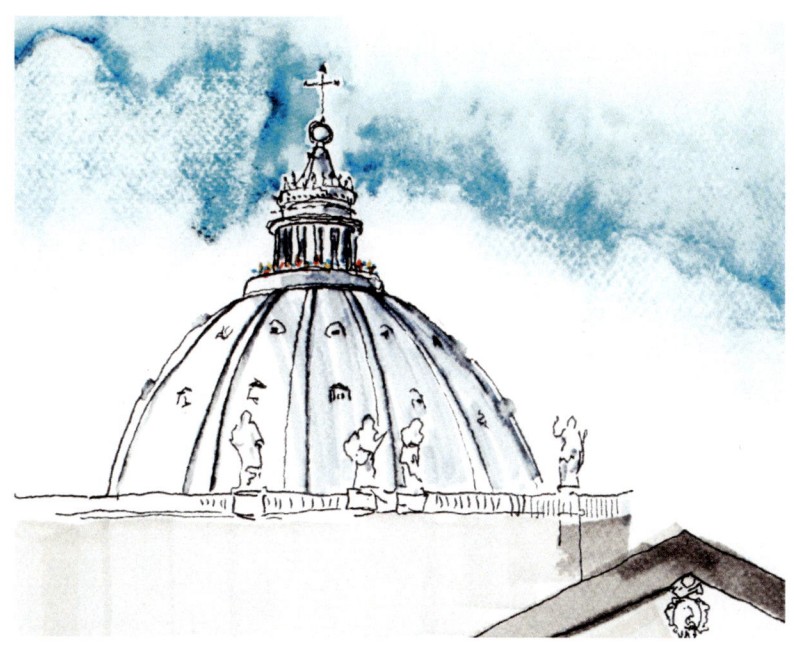

People in the Cupola

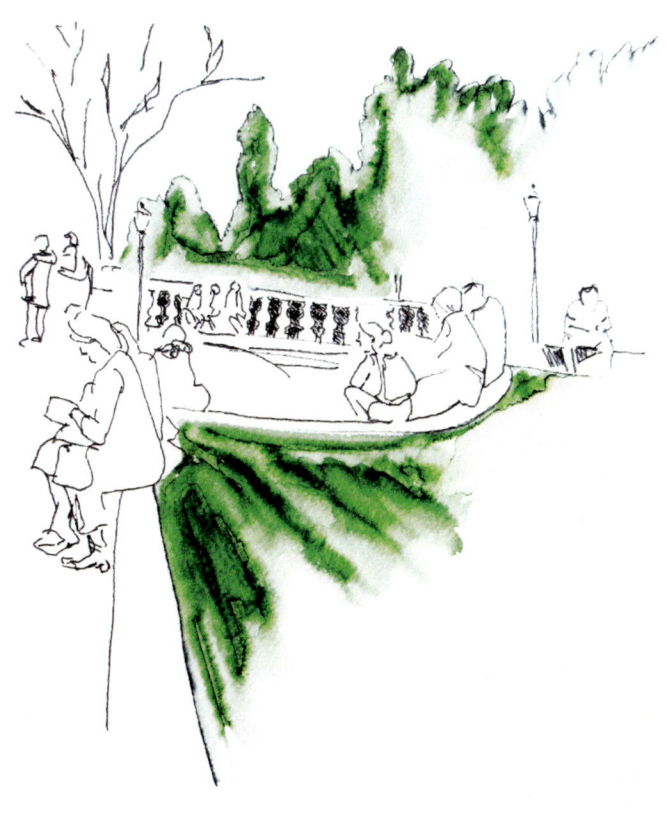

Villa Borghese Visitors

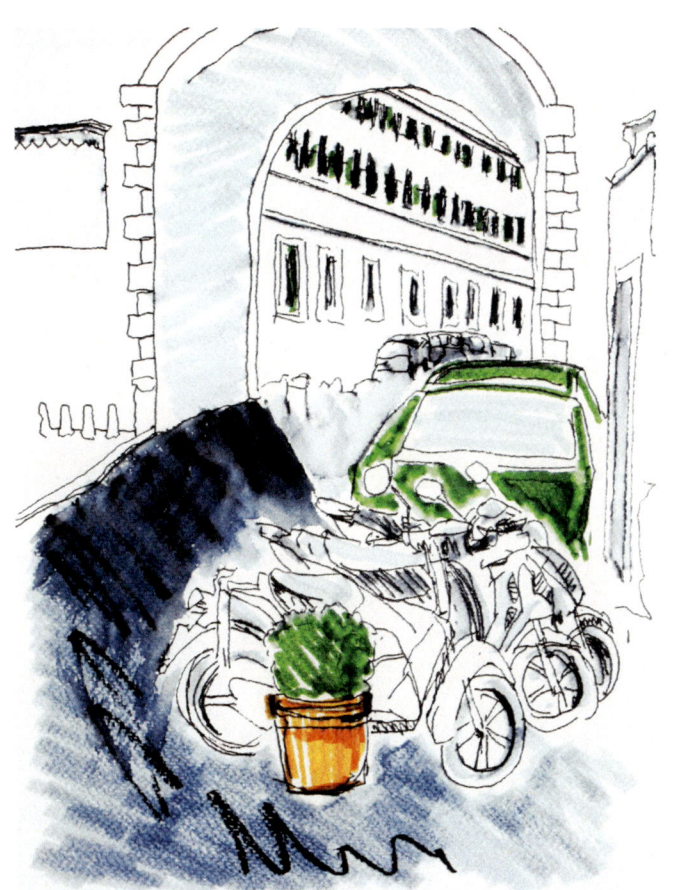

Cycles

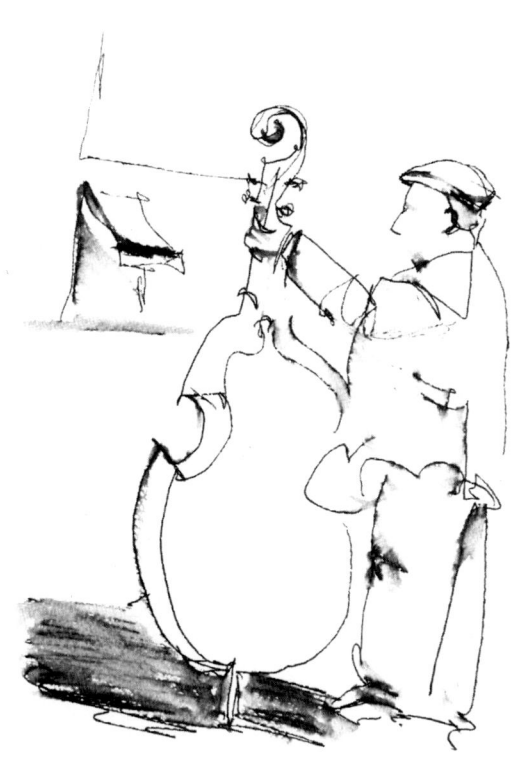

Noon in the Piazza

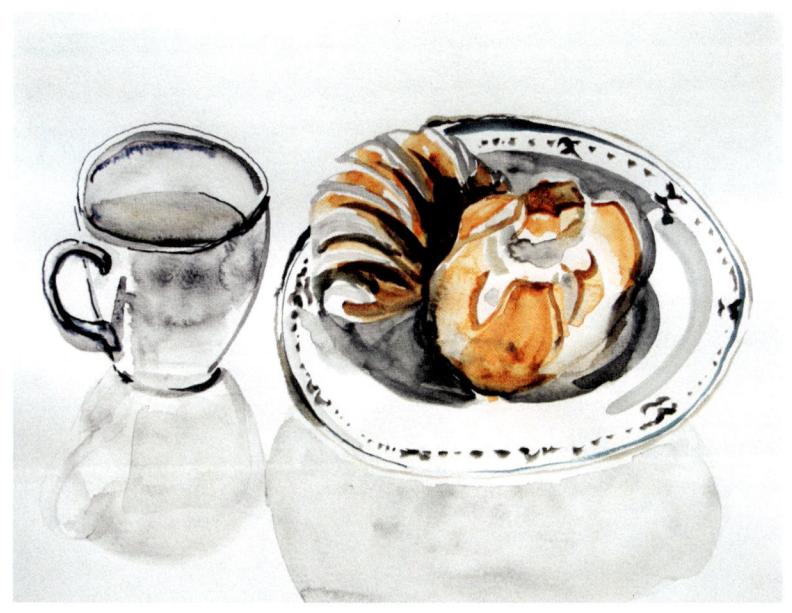

Panini

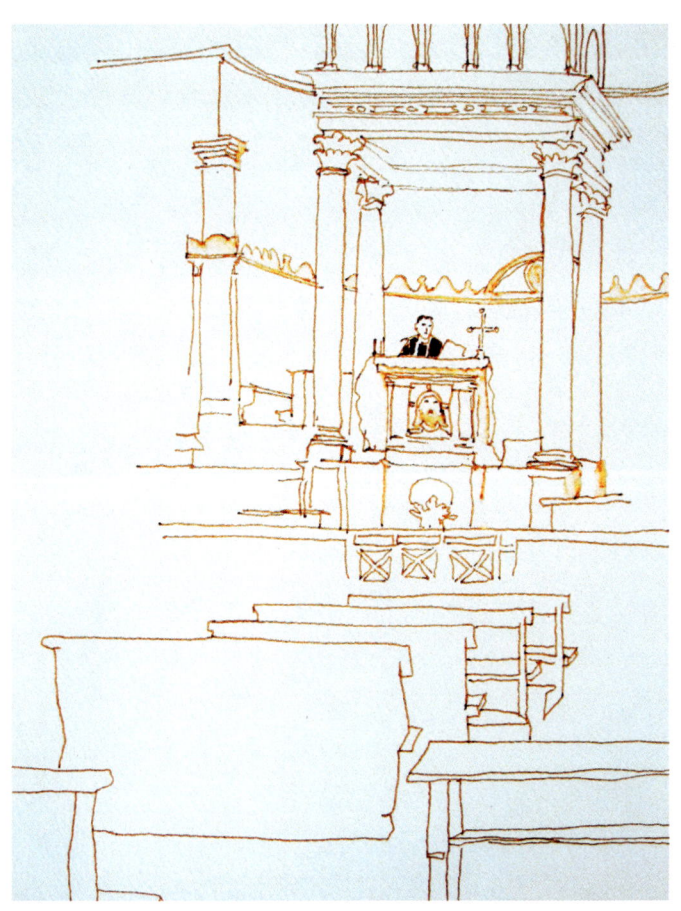

Monday Night Mass

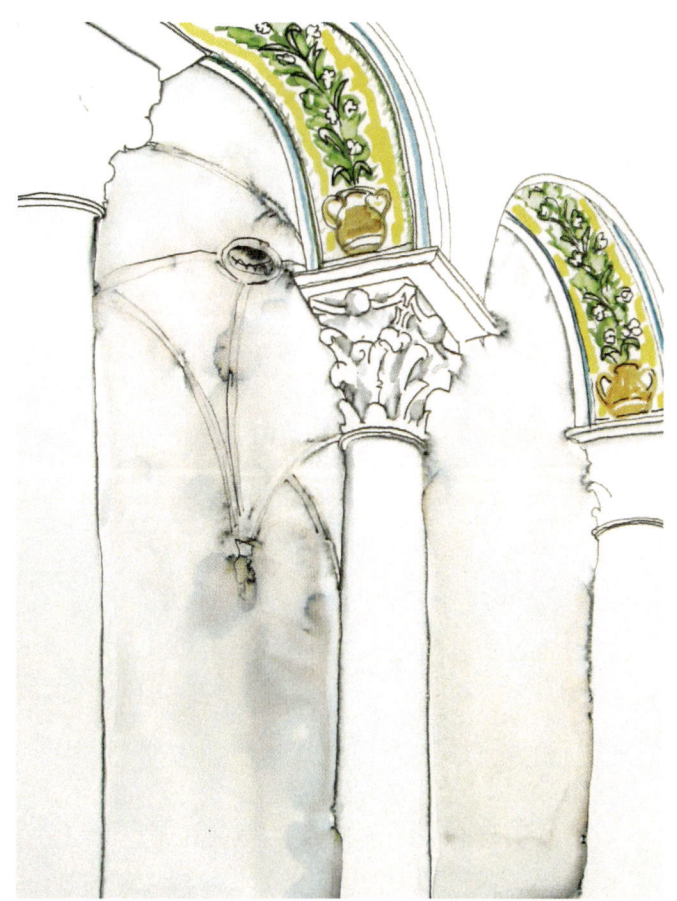

Sunday Evening Mosaics

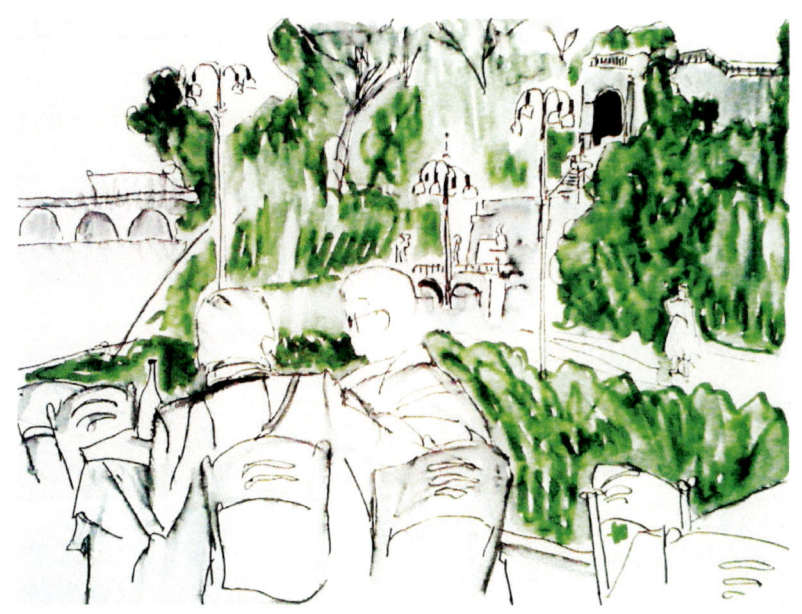

Edge of the Borghese Gardens

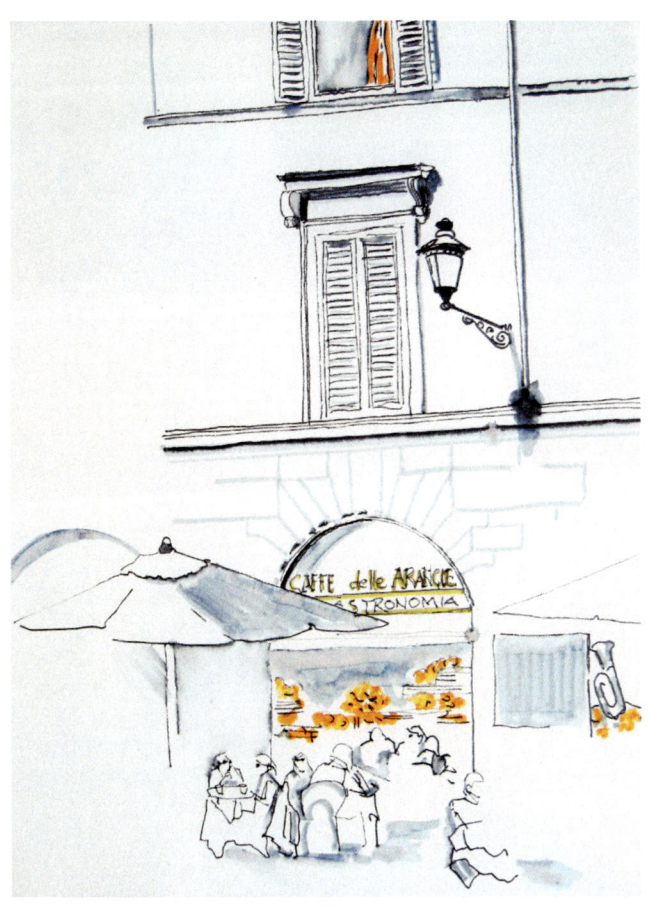

Neighborhood Fresh Orange Juice

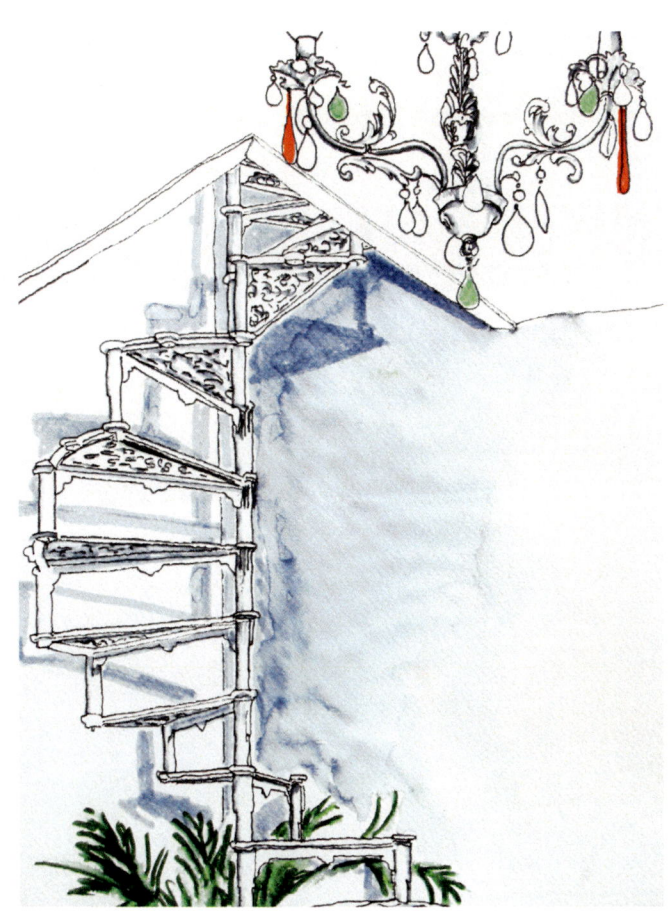

Our Entry Hall

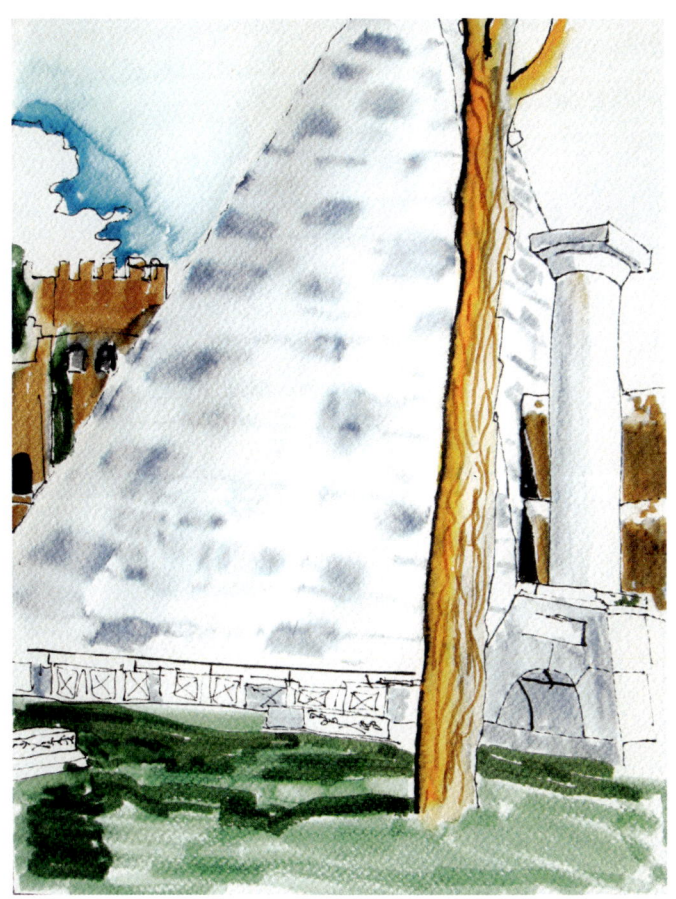

Rome's Pyramid

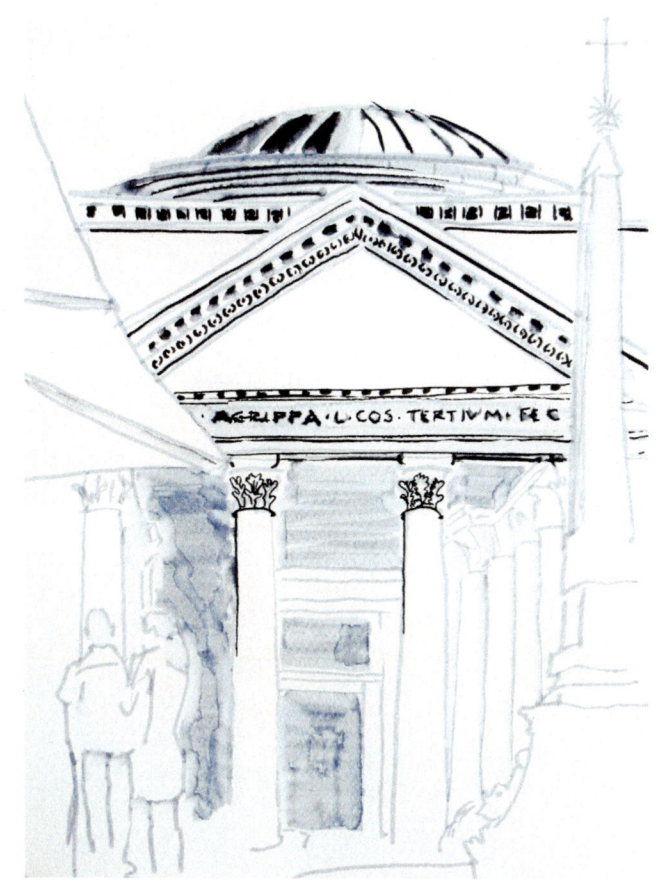

Pantheon #2

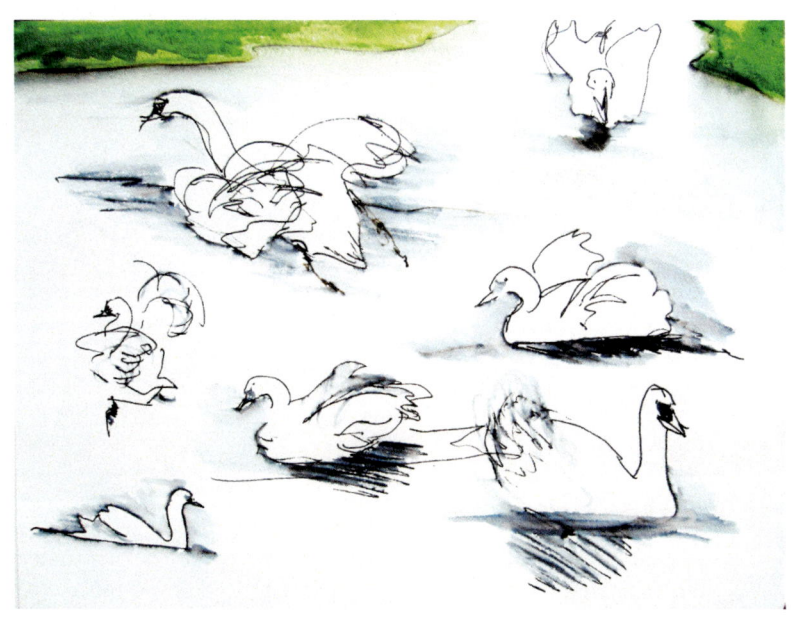

Life Drawing at the Villa Pamphili

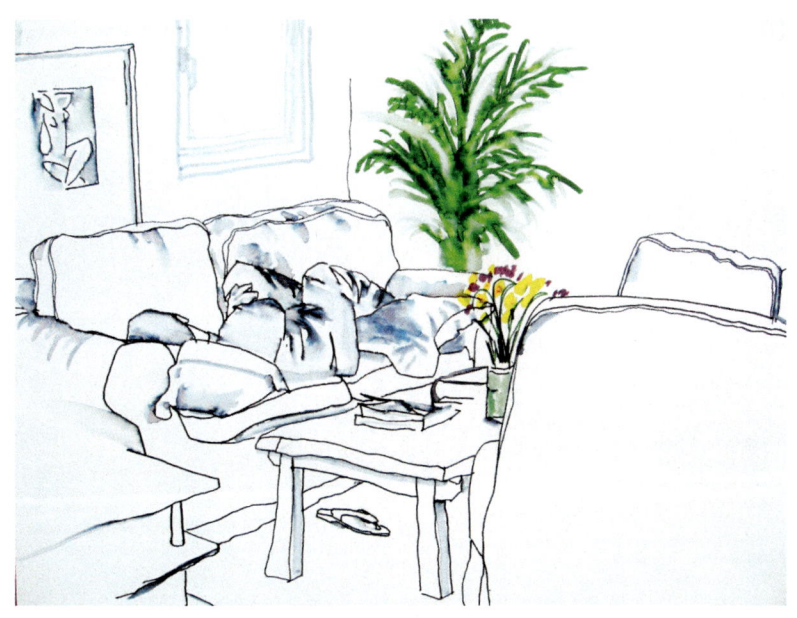

Life Drawing at Casa Garibaldi

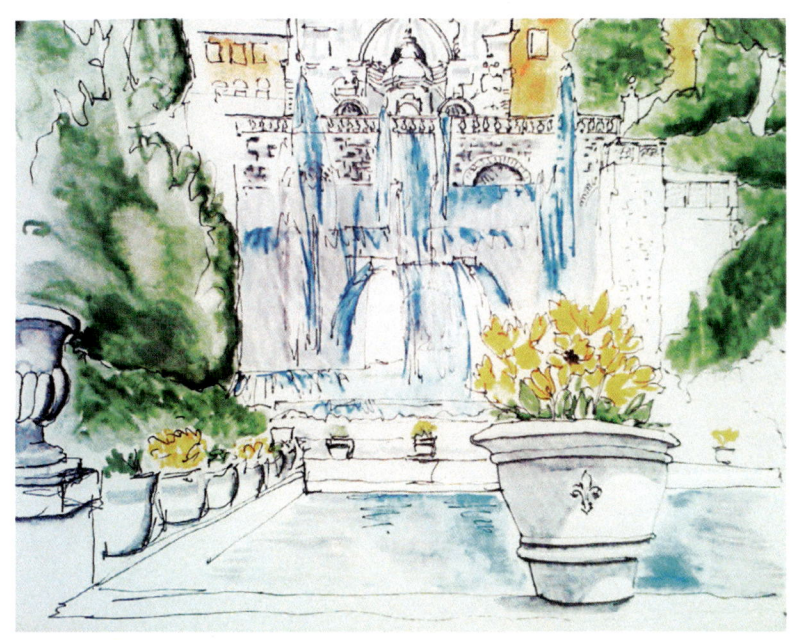

Waterworks at Villa d'Este

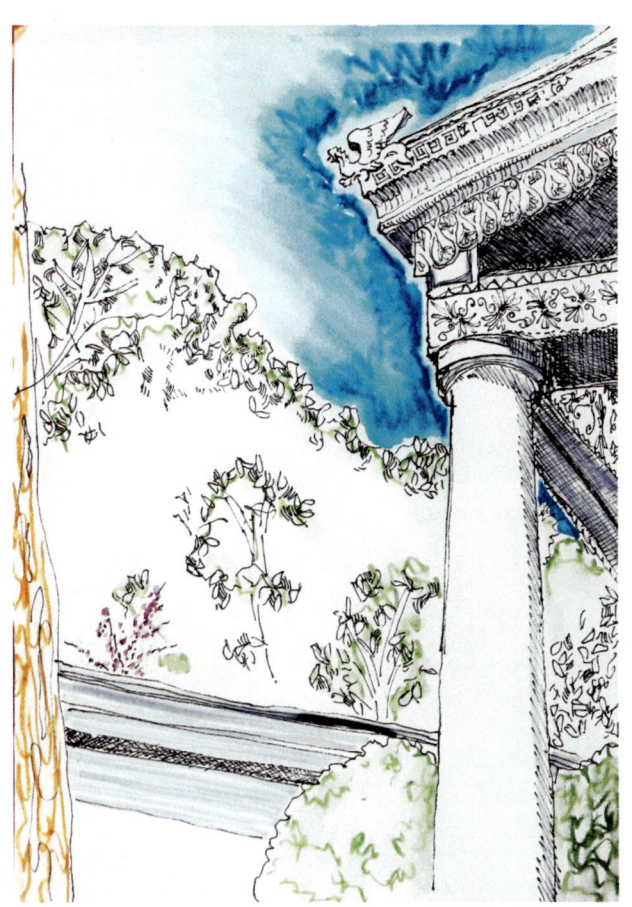

Etruscan Temple

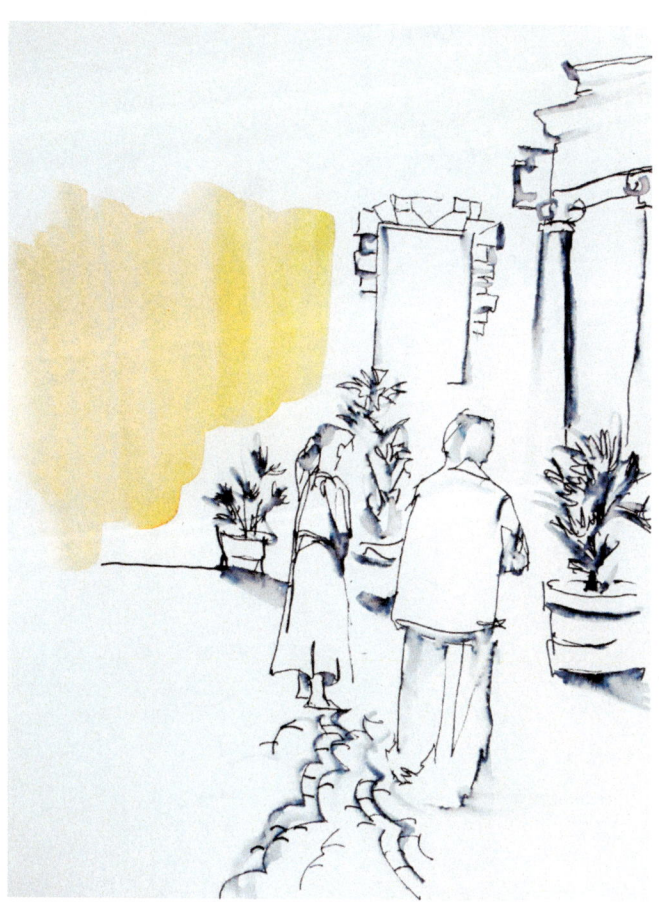

Piazza

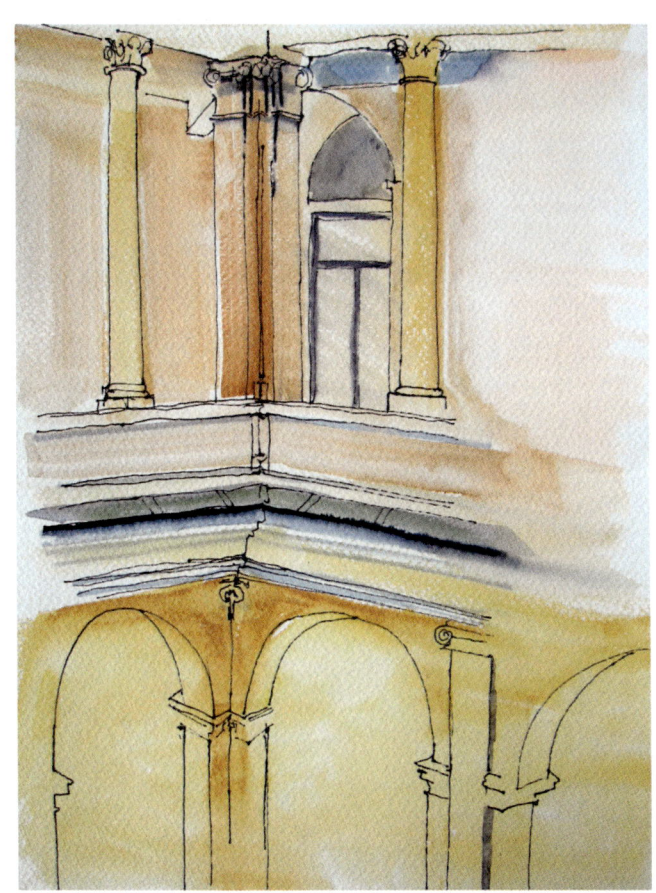

Two of Five Stories

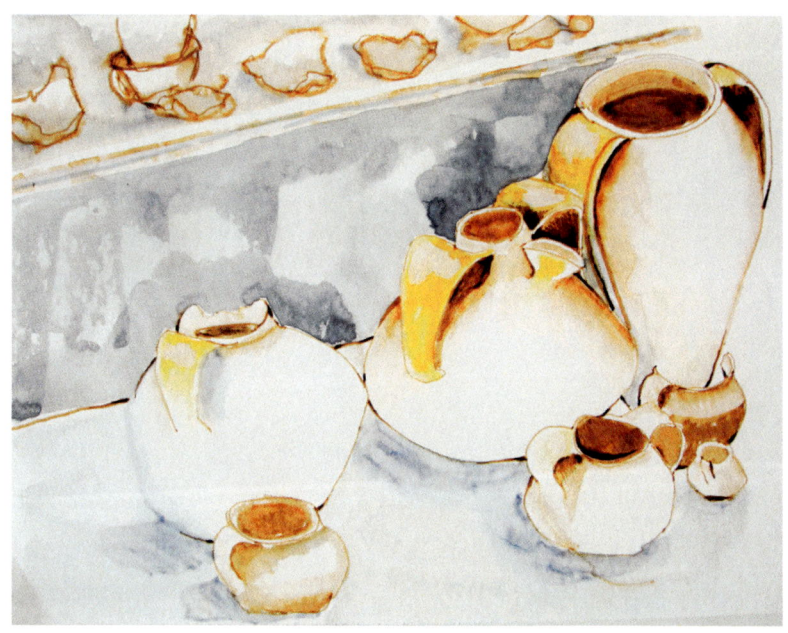

Terracotta

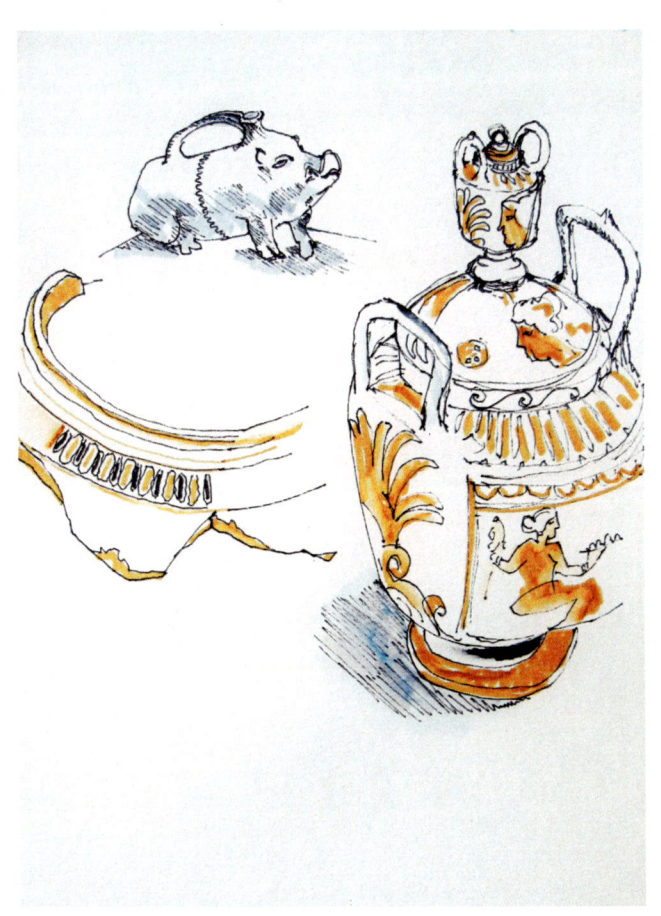

Etruscan Pottery

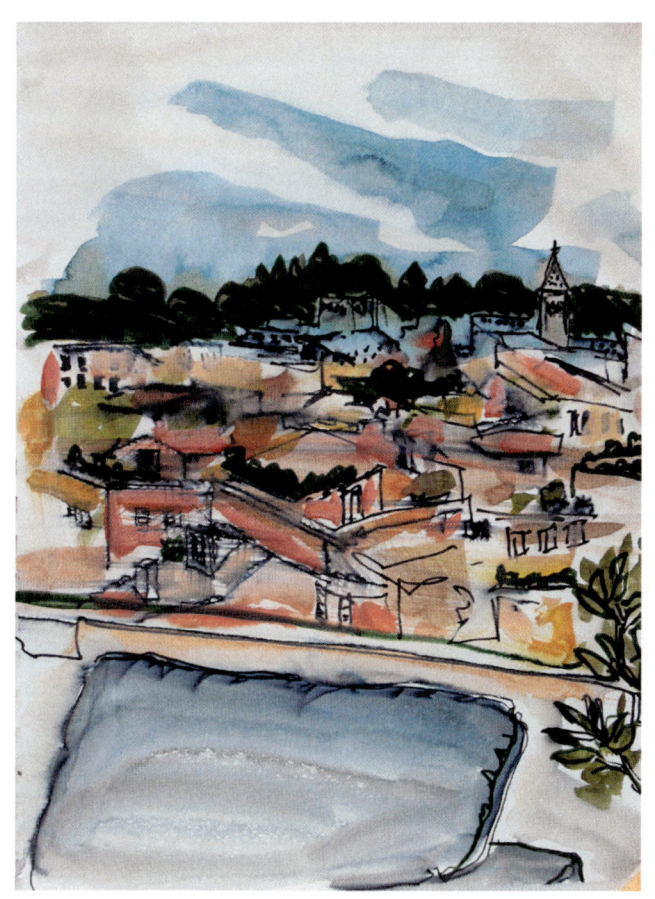

Roof Sofa

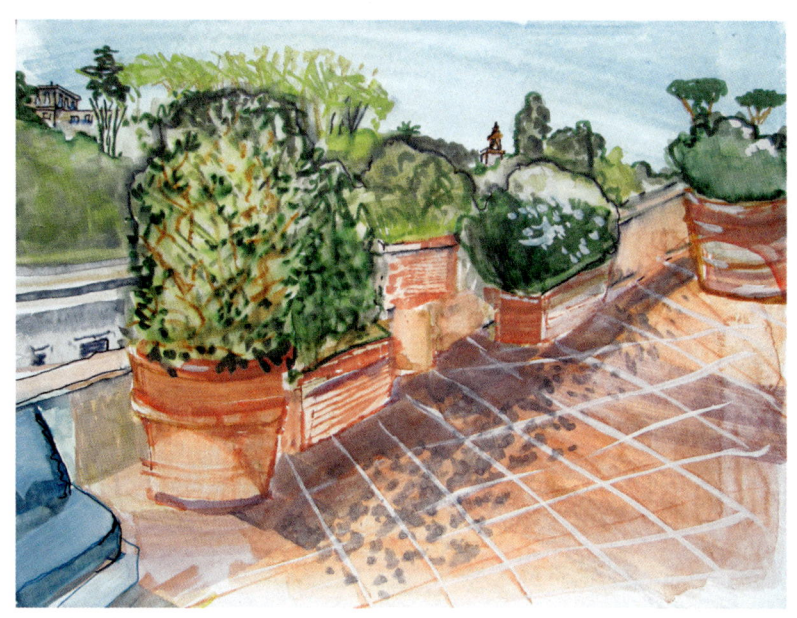

Roof Sofa 2

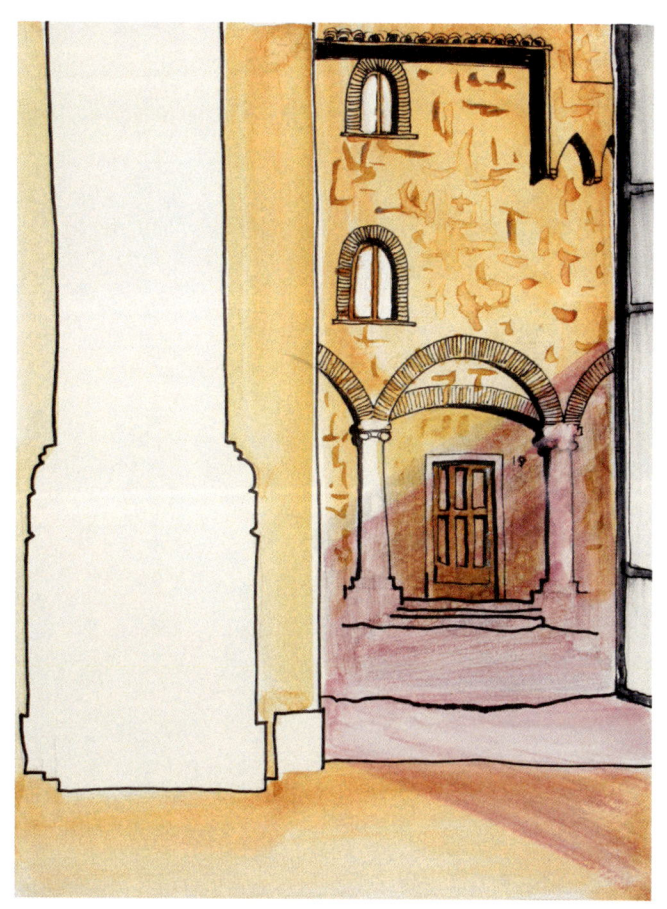

Columns from the Courtyard

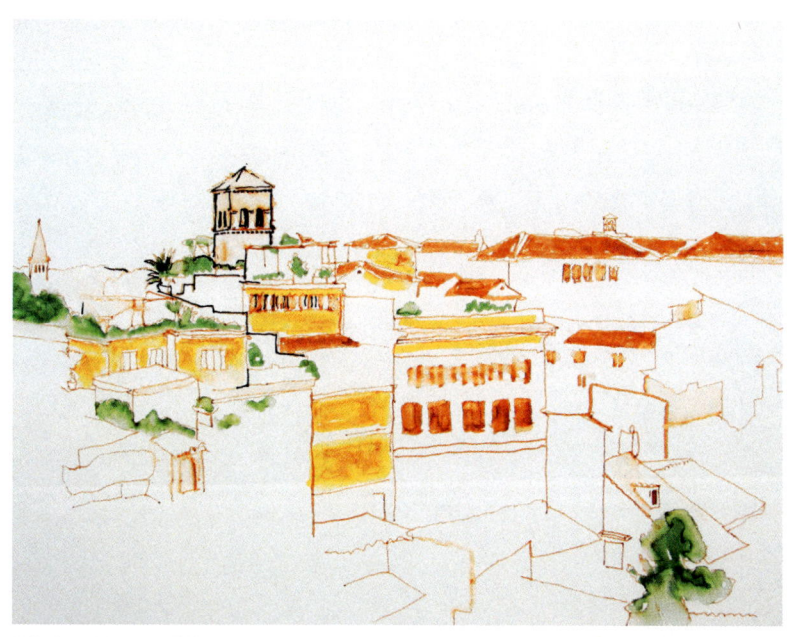

Living Room View #2

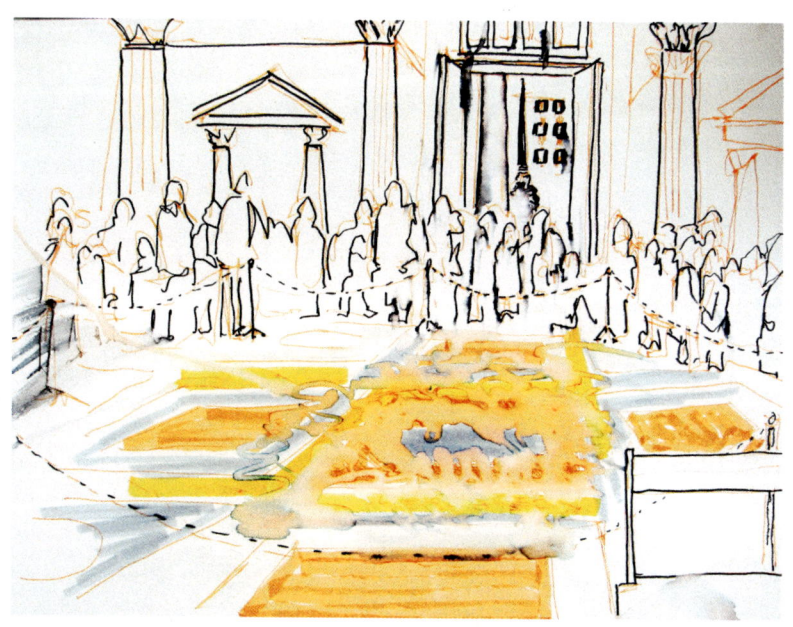

Pantheon in the Rain

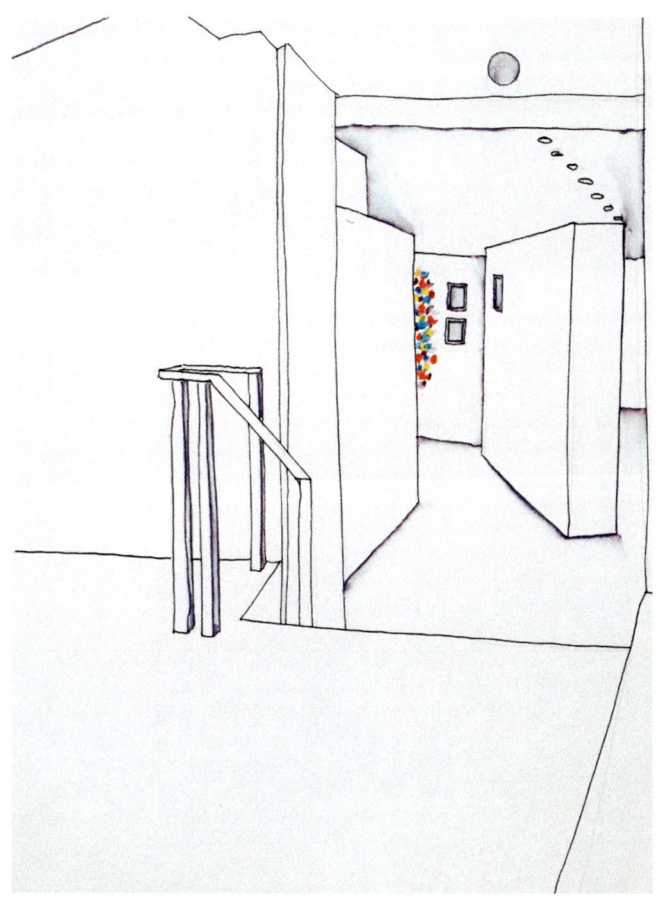

Mendini Retrospective

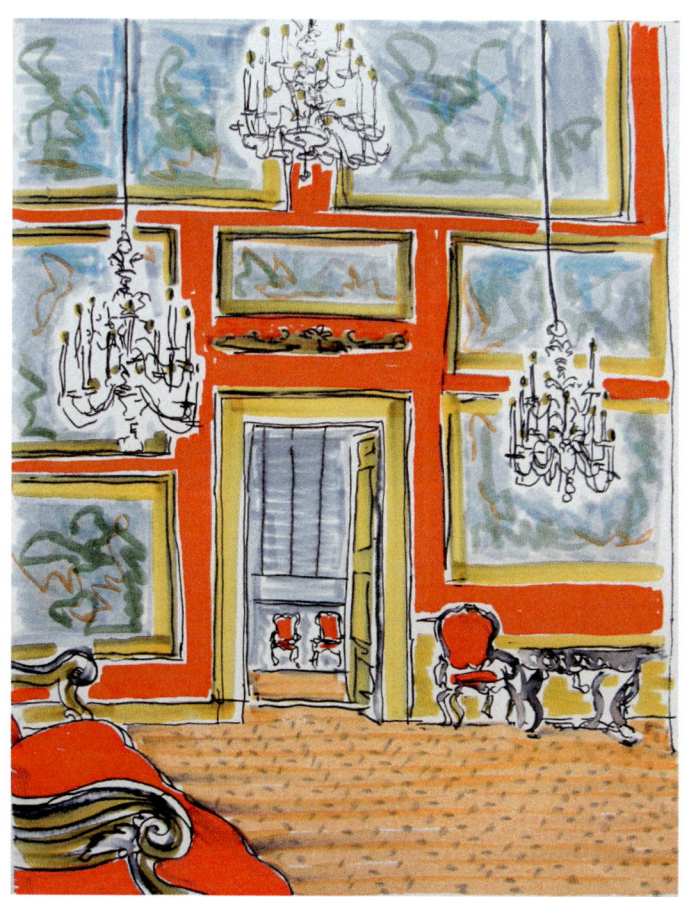

Palazzo

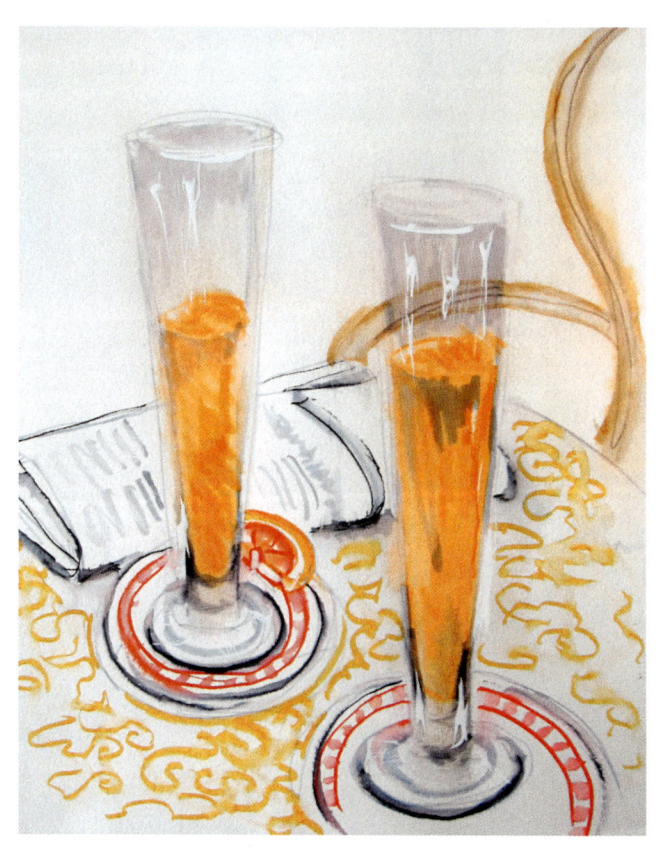

Due Spremute per Piacere

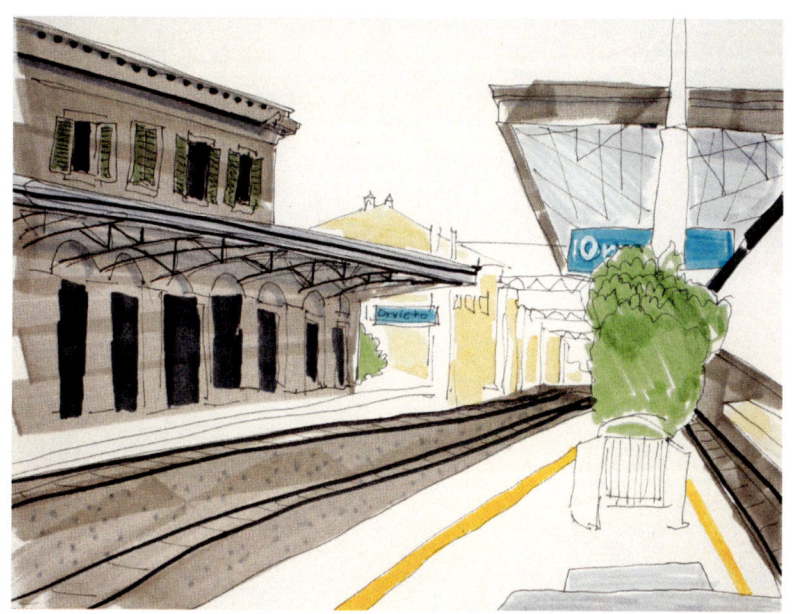

Day Trip

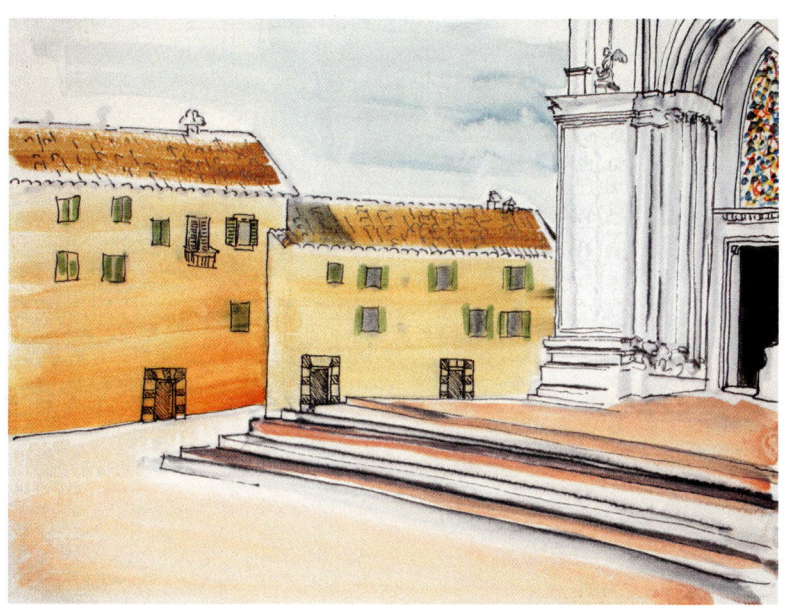

Orvieto

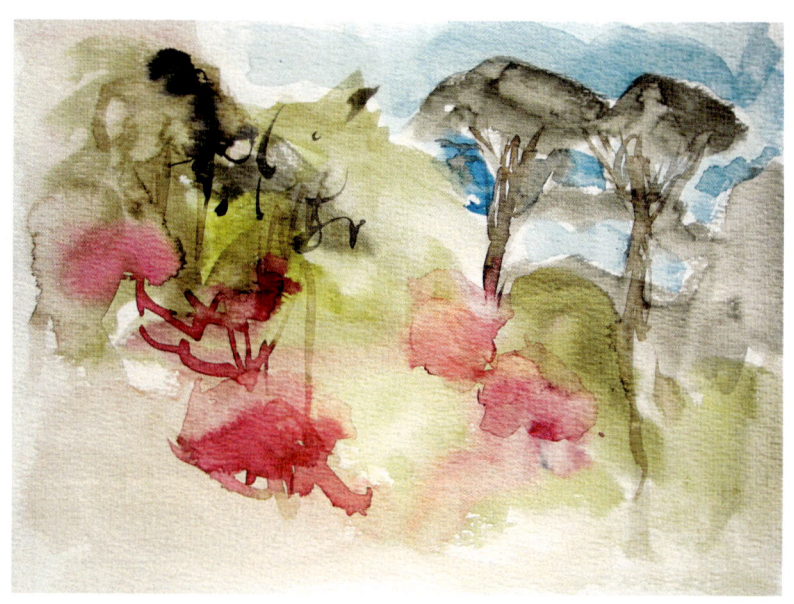

Judas Trees

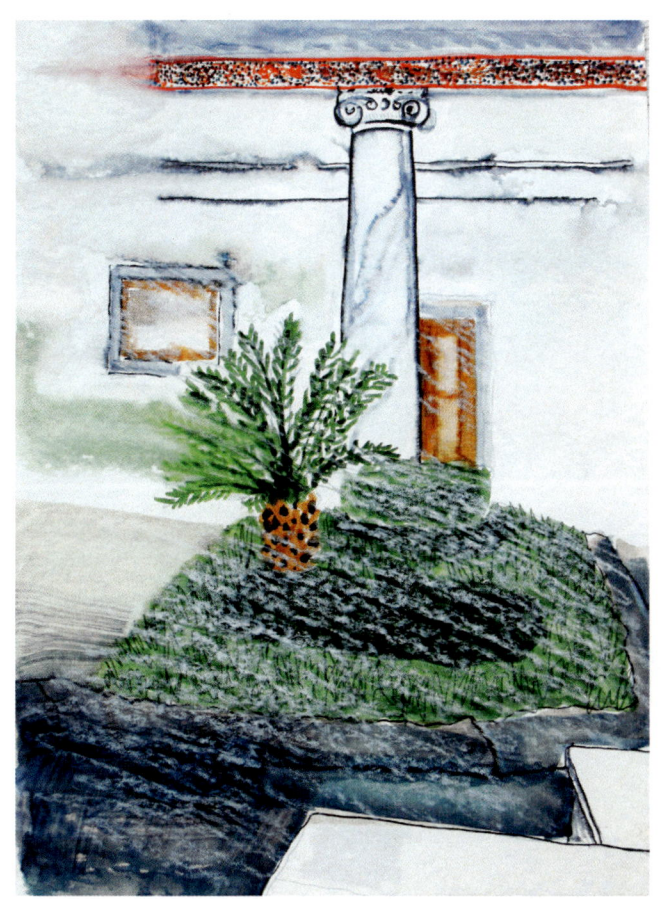

Santa Cecilia

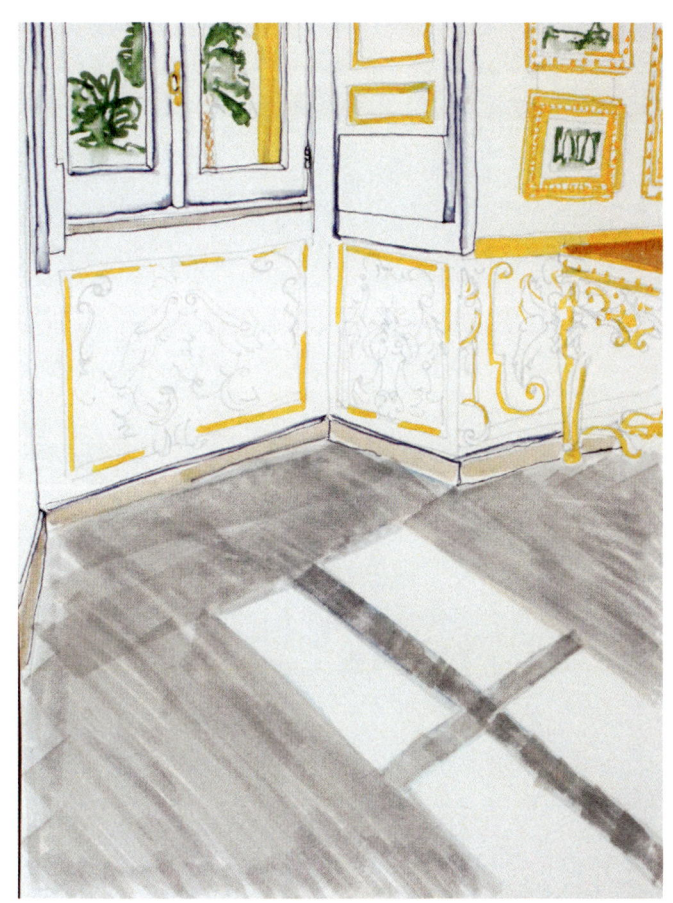

Sun in the Palazzo Corsini

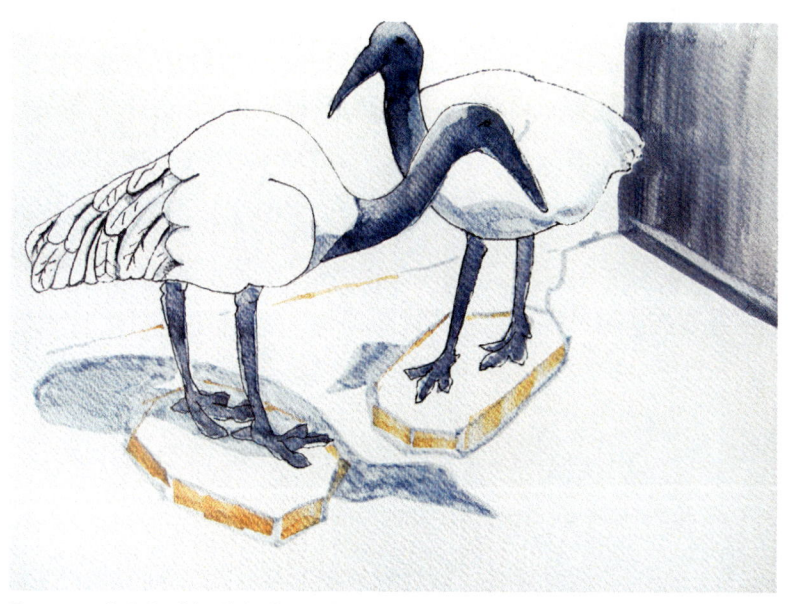

Bronze & Marble Ibis from Pompeii

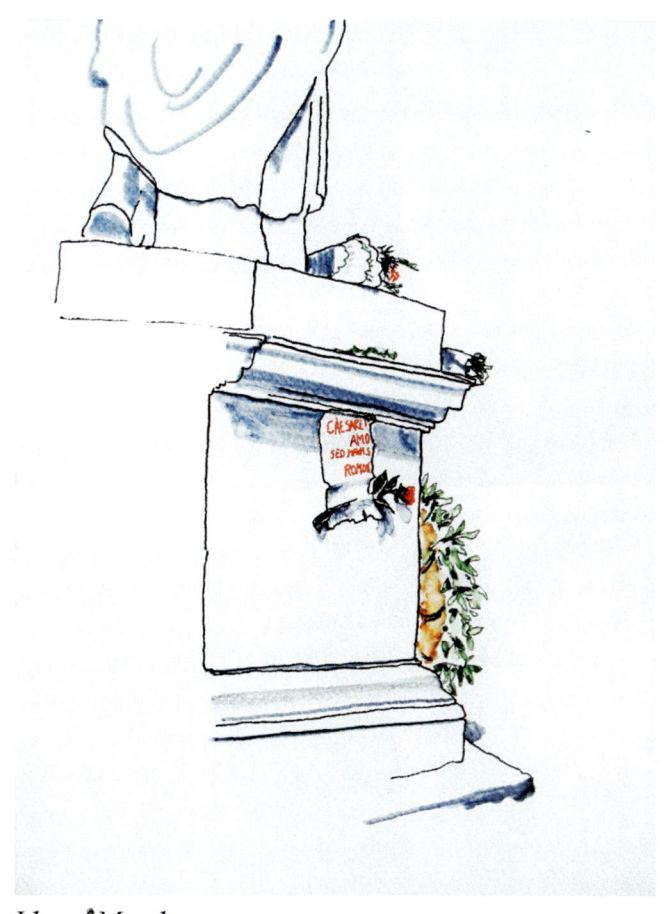

Ides of March

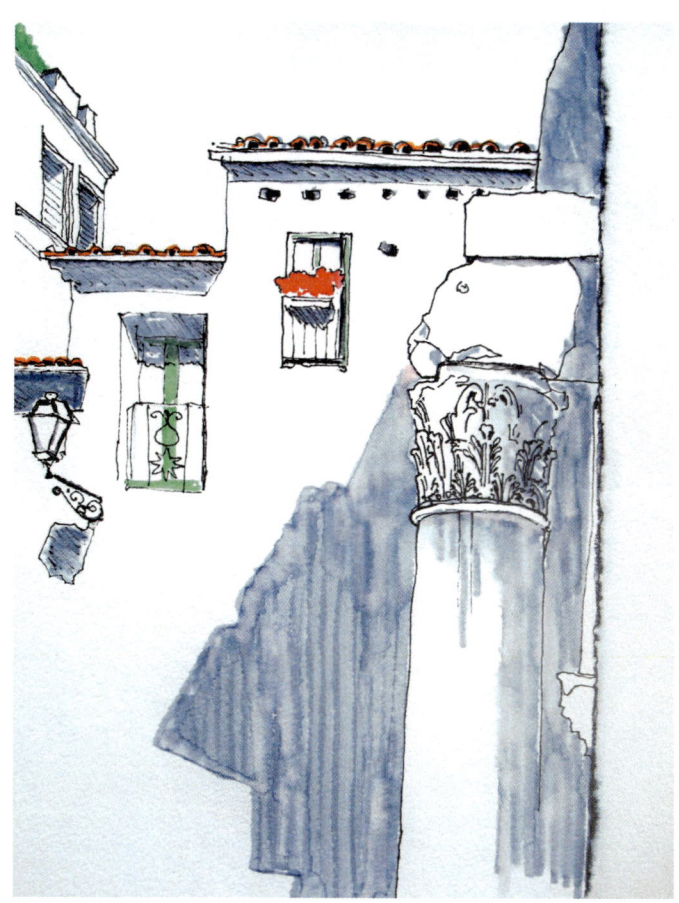

Cyclamen & Corinthian

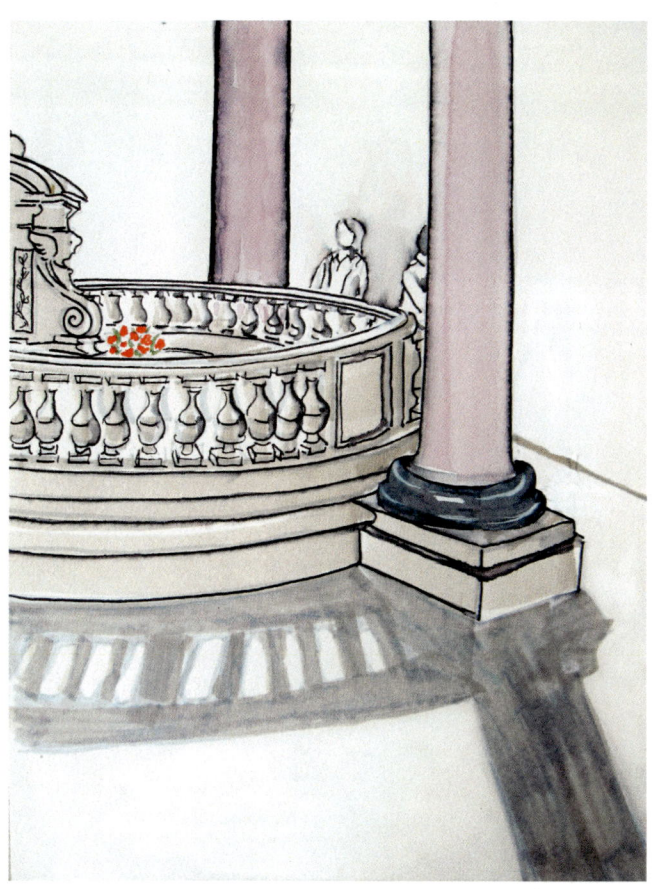

Purple Columns and Red Roses

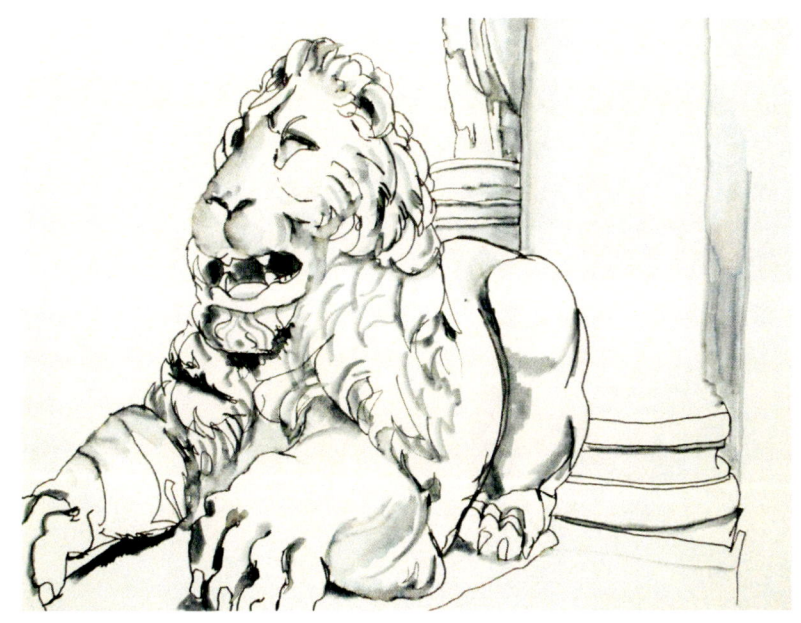

Capitolino Leone

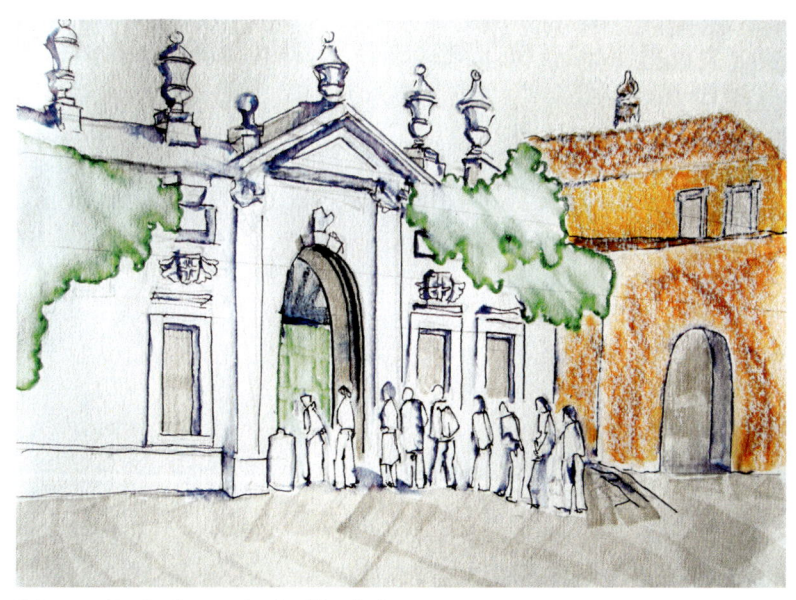

Line to Peek through the Keyhole

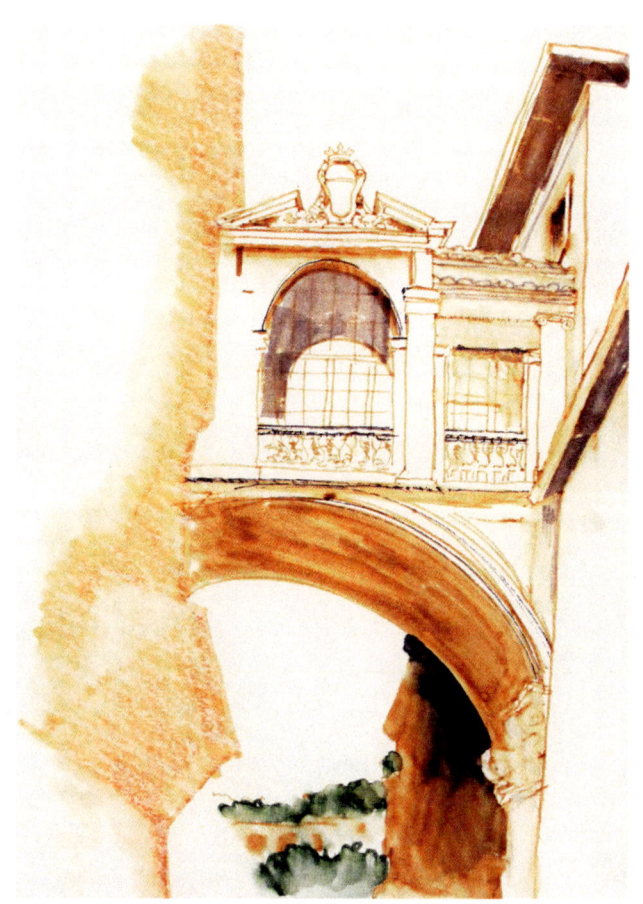

Under Restoration

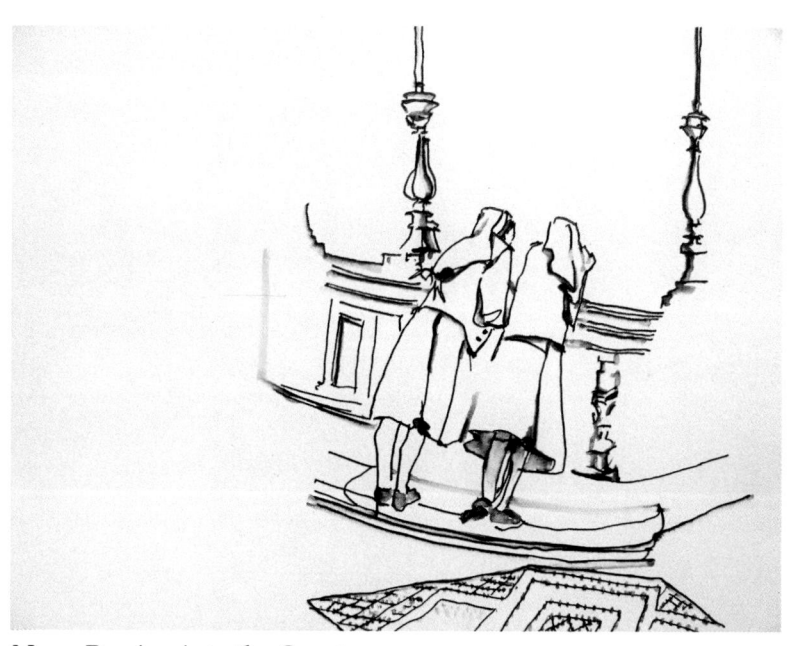

Nuns Peering into the Crypt

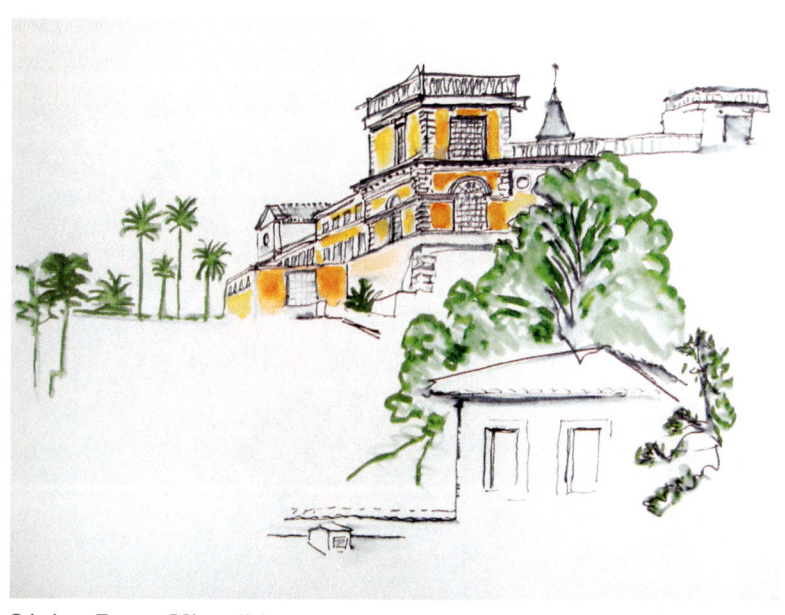

Living Room View #4

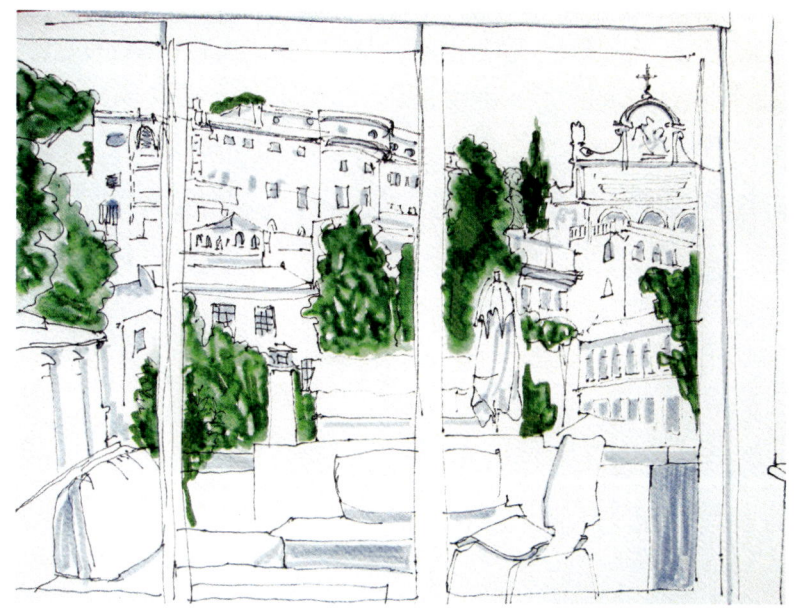

Living Room View #5

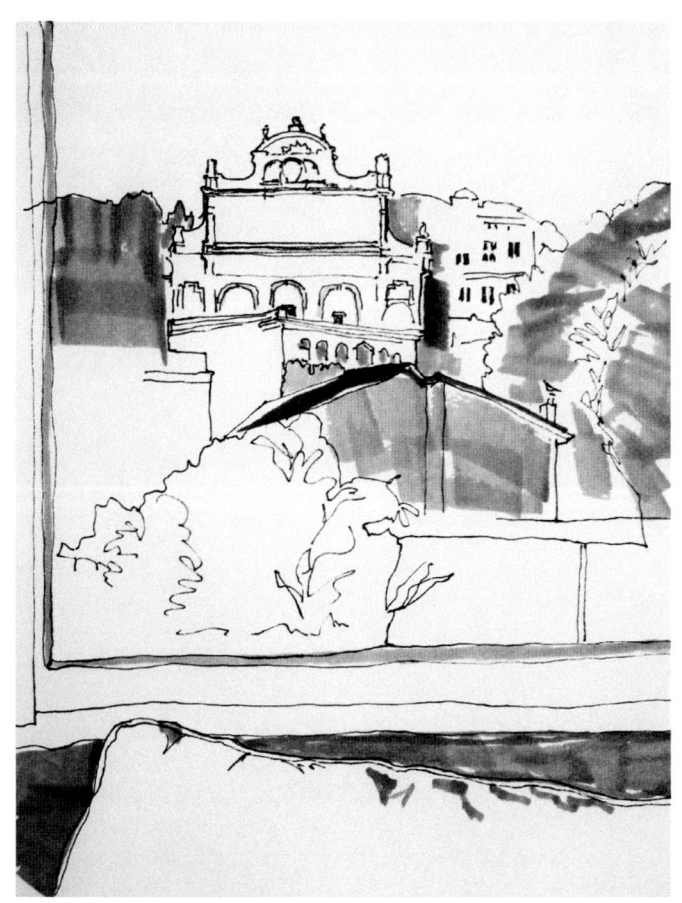

Living Room View #1

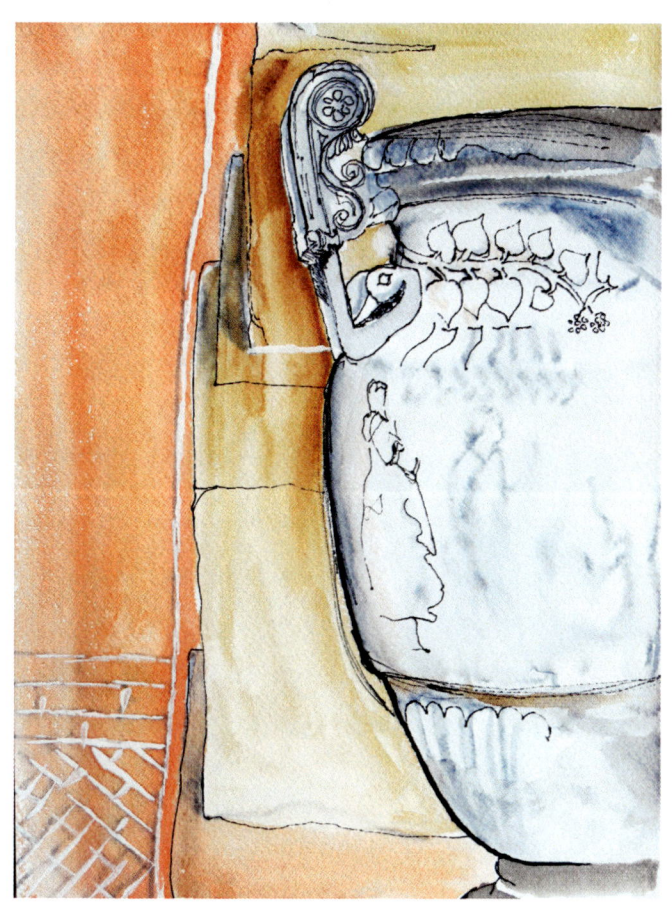

Marble Urn

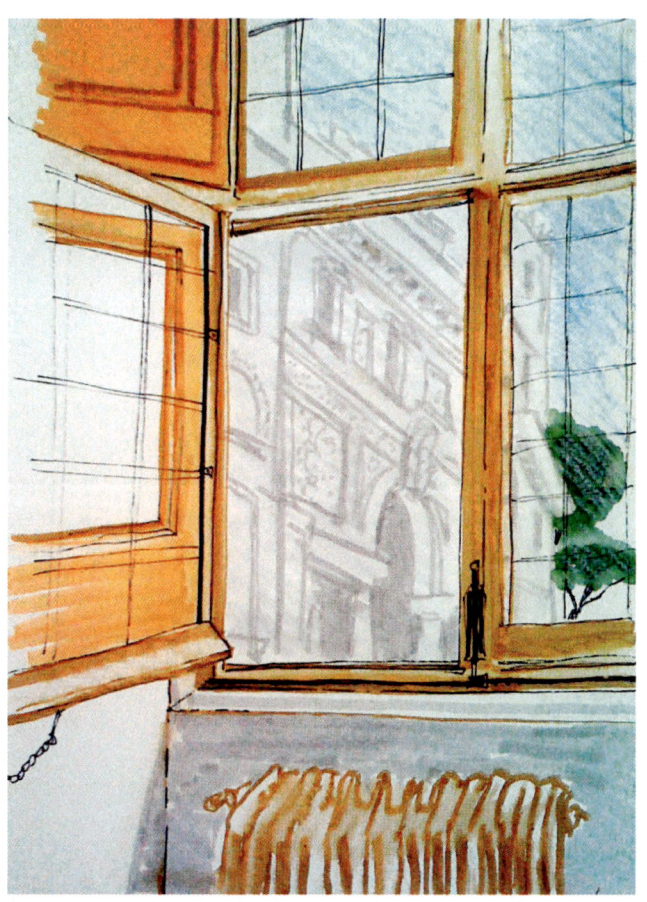

Lunch View, Villa Medici

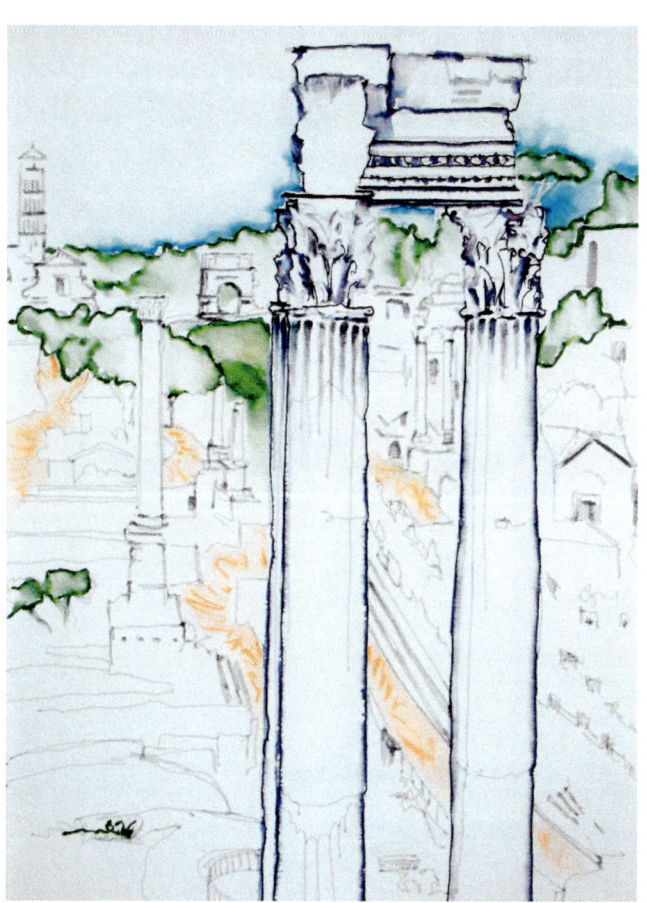

Path Through the Forum

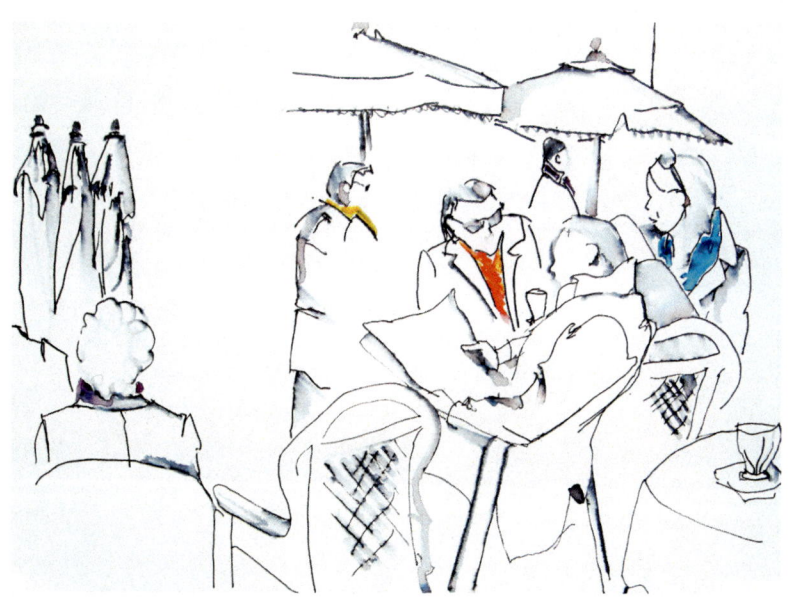

Scarves

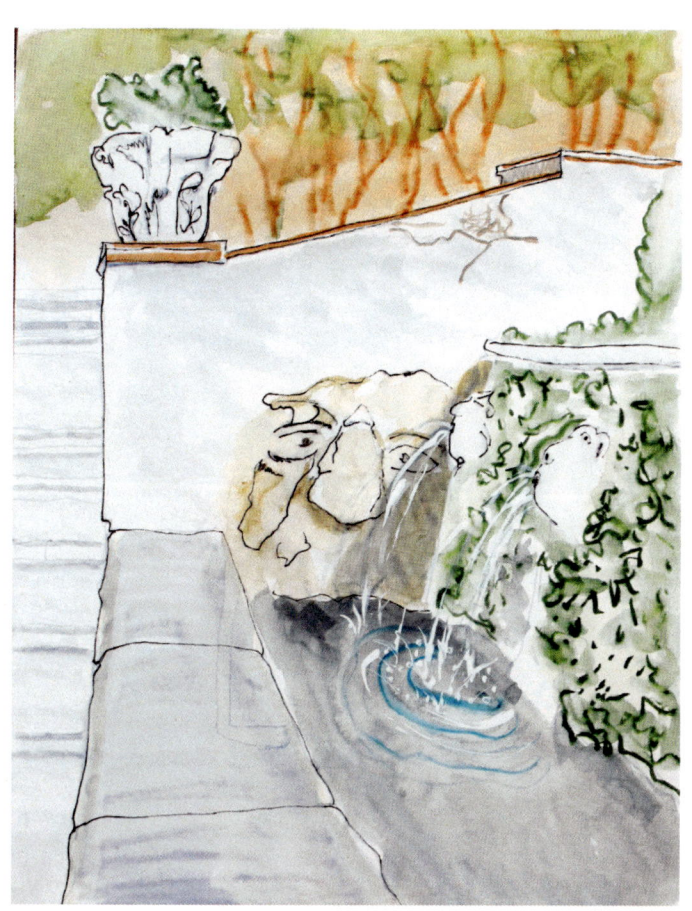

Serious Whimsy at Villa d'Este

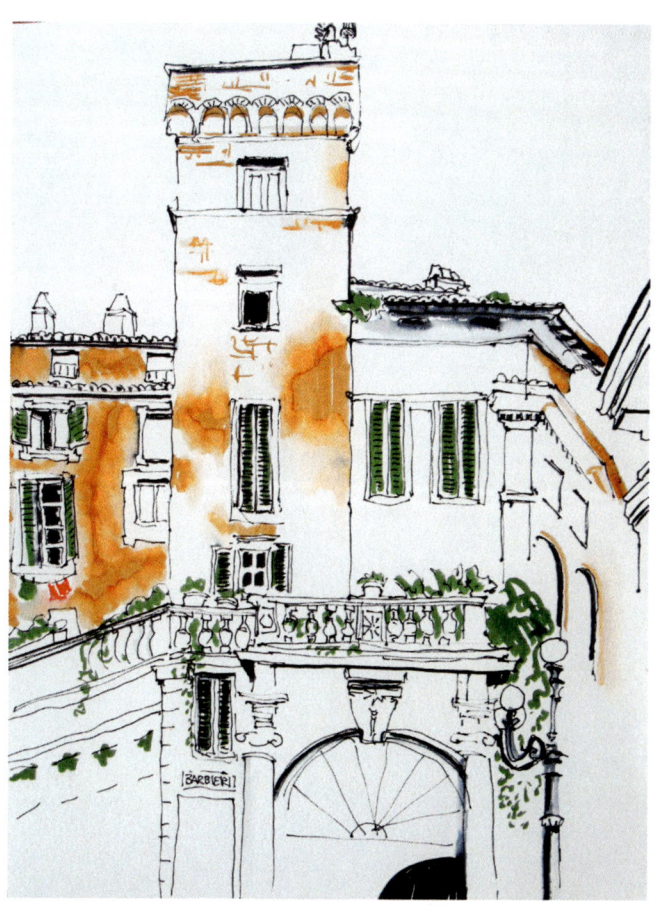

Torre della Scimmia

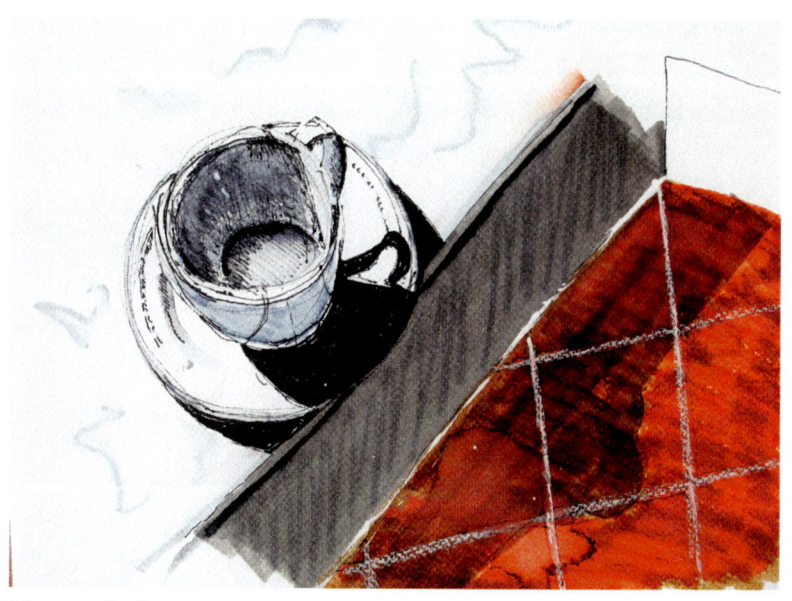

Tea on the Terrace

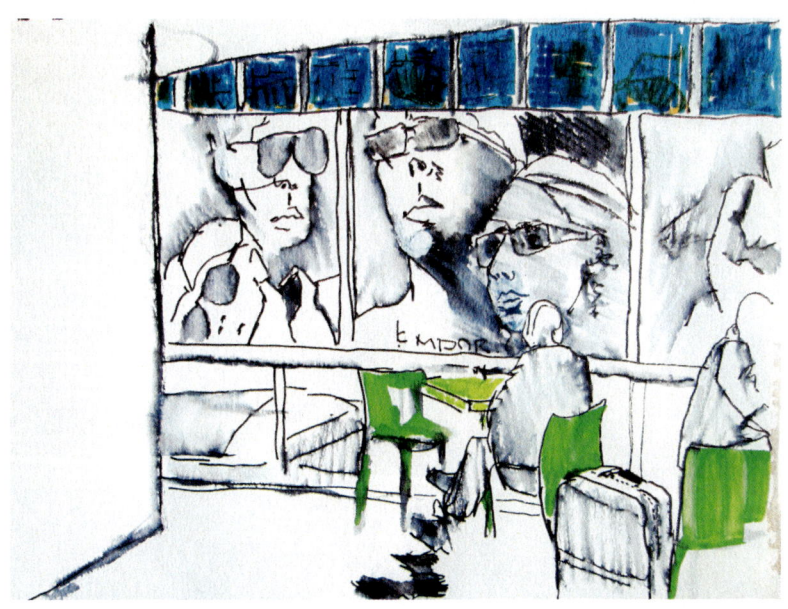

Sunglasses Billboards at Termini Station

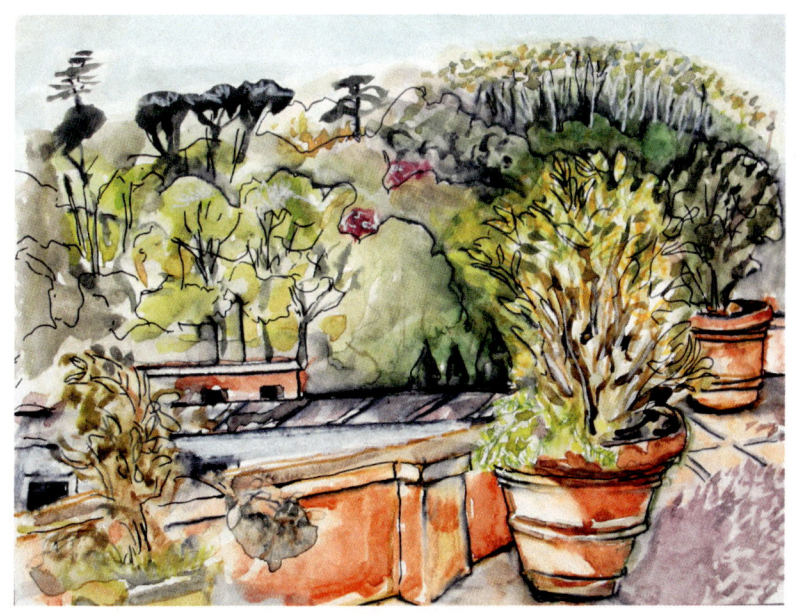

Too Nice a Day to Leave the Roof Terrace

Made in the USA
Las Vegas, NV
28 September 2022

56100869R00079